While I Am Sleeping

Written by Malaika Rose Stanley
Illustrated by Rachael Saunders

PEARSON

ISBN-13: 978-0-328-83271-2
ISBN-10: 0-328-83271-5

14   19

While I am sleeping and
tucked in my bed
at nighttime some people
are working instead.

The bakers make bread, chocolate cookies and pies,

and gingerbread people with
buttons and eyes.

While I am sleeping and tucked in my bed
at nighttime some people are working instead.

The garage attendant pumps gasoline
and the janitor dusts and scrubs everything clean.

While I am sleeping and
tucked in my bed
at nighttime some people
are working instead.

Brave firefighters put out
hot flames with a hose,
and doctors take care of
sick patients who doze.

While I am sleeping and tucked
in my bed
at nighttime some people are
working instead.

Street cleaners sweep sidewalks
and empty the trash,
and security guards watch over
the cash.

While I am sleeping and tucked
in my bed
at nighttime some people are
working instead.

Ambulance drivers with sirens
and lights
rush to help people all through
the night.

While I am sleeping and tucked
in my bed
at nighttime some people are
working instead.

Delivery drivers in trucks and
in vans
drop off papers and food in
packets and cans.

While I am sleeping and tucked
in my bed
at nighttime some people are
working instead.

When they are tired and need a
quick break,
they run to the diner for coffee
and cake.

While I am sleeping and
tucked in my bed
at nighttime some people
are working instead.

Market sellers pick up fish
and fresh meat
and boxes of fruit that
taste oh-so-sweet.

While I am sleeping and tucked
in my bed
at nighttime some people are
working instead.

Grocery store workers fill
up the shelves,
all laughing and
joking amongst
themselves.

While I am sleeping and tucked
in my bed
at nighttime some people are
working instead.

At stations and airports,
taxis wait in a row,
and the drivers take people
where they want to go.

While I am sleeping and
tucked in my bed
at nighttime some people
are working instead.

But when I wake up, bright
and early each day,
the night workers are
snoozing and snoring away.